T H E
HAWAIIAN
LUAU BOOK

BY LEE AND MAE KEAO

BESS PRESS, INC.
P.O. Box 22388
Honolulu, HI 96822

Many mahalos to those who contributed their cherished recipes, ideas, time, enthusiasm and support to this book.

Ann Rayson, Editor
Missy Blalack-McClendon, Artist
Marlene Bell
The Keao Ohana (family)
Susan Green
Levi Ezell, AAC, CEC, CCE
Bishop Museum, Honolulu, Hawaii
DOLE Foods

Printed in the United States of America

LIBRARY OF CONGRESS CATALOG CARD NUMBER: 87-92275

Keao, Mae and Lee
    The Hawaiian Luau Book
Honolulu, Hawaii: Bess Press, Inc.
    72 Pages

ISBN: 0-935848-59-2

Table Of Contents

Aloha Friends,

From the true Hawaiian — polite, warm and free spirited — was the aloha spirit born. It's a matter of the heart, a state of mind. It is a blessing. It is felt and experienced. It lingers.

The aloha spirit is not for us to own but something to be shared. That is why we present these ideas and guidelines to enable you to create your own enchanted tropical party.

There are as many different ideas for a luau as there are people. By using these suggestions as a basis for your planning, you can draw on your individuality to bring personal touches to your party. Basic patterns for the luau are presented, new twists may be added. This is your special forte as a host or hostess with a true love of entertaining.

No amount of time, money or effort can produce the truly essential ingredient for a successful luau — the special feeling of aloha.

Let us hear from you.

Mae and Lee

IN THE BEGINNING
THERE WAS THE LUAU

Hawaii was born from the sea, far from the human eye. Mighty volcanoes in the ocean floor spewed molten lava and rock upward with towering columns of smoke and great clouds of steam. And when the eruptions subsided, the cooled magma formed new mountains, piercing the water's surface and forming Hawaii.

Since this wondrous beginning, nothing has influenced Hawaiian culture as dramatically as its relationship with the sea.

The new paradise beckoned across the Pacific to the islanders of Tahiti. Guided by the heavens, the movement of the ocean currents, and the seasonal flights of birds with their incredible natural instincts, the early Tahitian voyagers crossed the vast span of deep salt water to their new island home more than a thousand years ago.

The main cargo carried in their great canoes was food — food not only for the perilous journey but, more importantly, for the new crops they would cultivate as Hawaii's first settlers. They guarded the coconut, bananas, breadfruit, taro and sweet potatoes zealously and sacredly, sustaining themselves primarily on the excess body fat they had purposely gained for the long voyage.

The rich brown earth of the Hawaiian Islands did not disappoint them. It offered up in great abundance the transplanted fruits and vegetables.

There was much starving and sacrifice before the new harvests were reaped. But this Polynesian people — strong, healthy and handsome — were not far removed from their origin and they flourished in the warm and sunny climates.

Discipline, skill and hard work produced bountiful crops in the near perfect climate. The robust bronze-skinned people supplemented their daily fare with seaweed and fish from the cobalt blue Pacific.

Fishermen exchanged their catch for taro root (pounded into poi), fruit and vegetables. These early exchanges established eating habits still in existence among the Hawaiian people. "Fish and poi" is spoken of in near reverence by the lovers of Island food.

The bounty of land and sea wasn't taken for granted. The people were grateful and they showed it by offering up prayers to their gods before eating.

The nature of the gods, though powerful and awesome, carried the natural motivations of man. The Hawaiians, associating the closeness they felt for one another when their opus (bellies) were being filled,

5

concluded that man and god could also feel better rapport if they ate together.

Feasts of early Hawaii (and sometimes even ordinary meals) conveyed a sense of close communication between man and the gods. These feasts were more than a ritualistic offering of food to the spirits. It was also believed the gods were present throughout the meal, thus creating a closer relationship between them and man and making them more receptive to man's requests.

And it followed that the people, eager to please and impress their gods, carefully chose the foods that would appease the spiritual appetites.

Kalua pig, baked in the ground, was considered a favorite of the gods and preferable to fowl. However, moa (chicken) was once used as a very specific food offering. A speckled fowl reputedly would conquer insanity, a Plymouth Rock would cure a sickly infant.

Limu kala (seaweed) was believed to release man from wrongdoings. Ti leaves, spread as tablecovering, elicited protection from the gods and cleansed man from contamination.

The Makahiki was a major time of feasting and celebration. Food was cooked in an imu (underground oven), heated by lava rock and covered with fresh banana leaves. This glorious season of fun, dancing, games, contests and much eating began with thankful prayers to the god Lono for blessing the people with the abundance of the land and sea.

The introduction of Christianity to Hawaiians eventually deposed the gods; the symbolism of the food and the feast has been likewise diminished. Yet, when Hawaiians of today hold a luau, the spirit of old Hawaii remains.

KAMAAINA LUAU

The Hawaiian Way

The luau in Hawaii is usually a special feast, a celebration of a wedding, birthday, graduation, wedding anniversary or a family (Ohana) get-together. It's a time for fun, food, dancing and music.

Start your preparations when the idea first enters your mind. Get cousins, aunties and uncles together. Delegate jobs, based on the checklist in this book or one of your own. Get organized and stay organized so that no guesswork will linger near the actual luau time.

Decide when the group will gather on a regular basis to report progress. Correspond with guests to build their enthusiasm and expectation for the great event.

These planning sessions can also be potluck parties — extra opportunities to renew and strengthen family bonds.

Because the preparation and expense of a luau are considerable, ask family and friends to help by:

1. Gathering opihi from the rocks, catching fish and gathering seaweed.
2. Picking ti leaves, flowers, pineapple, bananas, sweet potatoes and flowers.
3. Assisting in the preparation, cooking and serving of the food (children and teenagers enjoy catering to the cousins, aunties and uncles for seconds) and with the cleanup.
4. Involving the children to give them the sense of family and benefitting from their endless energy and ideas. Remember that the aloha spirit is caught, not taught.
5. Securing entertainment well in advance but also allowing for impromptu entertainment by aunties who've become silly and children making mistakes.
6. Preparing the pig, imu or rotisseries.

Menu
Kalua Pig
Lomilomi Salmon
Chicken Luau
Chicken Long Rice
Fish in Ti Leaves
Poi and Steamed Rice
Poke Aku and Opihi
Baked Sweet Potato
Haupia
Fresh Pineapple
Banana Bread
Punch and Beverage

Decor

It's no problem to choose a setting and decorate for a luau in Hawaii. Everything is at arm's length. In the midst of tropical paradise, weather is the least consideration year around. Predictable and monotonously wonderful, the lure of the outdoors is an invitation and embrace.

Our party places are almost always outdoors and open to the sky by day, the heavens by night, the sea and regal mountains. The sites are caressed with balmy trade winds and blessed with swaying palms and soft moonlit evenings. Luaus in Hawaii are celebrated in extraordinary settings.

The day before the luau, erect a tent to accommodate the expected crowd. Set up tables.

Decor is traditional and easily gathered. After covering with butcher or tapa paper, spread fresh fern fronds on tabletops. Place ti leaves down the center lengthwise of the tables. Arrange whole pineapples, then fresh flower petals atop the ti leaves and ferns.

Cover tent poles and band stand with the greenery. For privacy, youngsters should attach coconut palm branches to a wooden frame built around the tent.

Place fresh flowers wherever you like.

In the land of real aloha, all the party decorations are already on hand!

Attire

Appropriate apparel for a party in paradise is one's best aloha shirt or muumuu. Many families have special tee shirts designed for the occasion with the O'hana (family) name printed on the back. This may be a good time to design one, perhaps adding a family crest.

Fresh flowers should abound in leis and hokus (woven head leis), often made by keikis (children) while tutus and tutu kanes (grandmas and grandpas) care for the little ones.

Imu
Hawaiian Underground Oven

(This ain't for sissies)

In preparing an imu, the following materials are required:

1. Kindling wood
2. Kerosene
3. Porous lava rocks in various sizes
4. Firewood, split in halves or quarters
5. Eight banana stumps, cut in two-foot sections, mashed and shredded
6. Banana and ti leaves
7. Twelve burlap sacks, cut to open flat
8. Two large canvas tarps
9. Two 6-foot square pieces non-galvanized chicken wire
10. Eight feet non-galvanized tie wire
11. Long-handled tongs
12. Workbench
13. Hawaiian rock salt
14. Two large pans
15. One 7-foot length of 2-inch pipe

Select a soft ground site where digging won't be difficult. The diameter and depth of the imu, as well as the cooking time, depend on the size and weight of the fully cleaned and dressed pig. A fifty-pound pig will take approximately two and one half to three hours cooking in a hole five feet across and gradually tapered to three feet in depth.

After the hole is dug, place the pipe vertically in the center of the hole; it should extend well above the rim of the hole. Lay kindling around the bottom of the pipe; sprinkle the wood with kerosene. Fill the hole with firewood, stacking crisscross around the pipe and up to the rim of the hole. Pile lava rocks on the wood, stacking them to form a pyramid.

Remove the pipe from the hole. Dampen a piece of burlap with kerosene, ignite and push down into center of the hole. Let the fire burn approximately two hours or until the wood is consumed and the rocks are red hot. When the rocks settle in the hole, remove any unburned wood and level the rocks.

Hint: Prepare the imu, to the point of lighting it, the day before you actually cook the pig. Protect the imu overnight by covering it with canvas. Light the fire when preparing the pig.

The pig must be completely cleaned and dressed. Cut it between both front legs and the rib cage to form pockets or cavities. Place the pig on a sheet of chicken wire. Sprinkle Hawaiian rock salt into the open cavities and abdominal areas. Stuff small red hot rocks in the abdominal and foreleg cavities. Tie all four legs together with tie wire; completely wrap chicken wire around pig and secure.

With rocks red hot and the pig ready for cooking, line the hole with shredded banana stumps, banana and ti leaves. Place pig in center of hole, its back on the bottom.

Additional foods such as sweet potatoes, poultry, fish and wild game may be cooked with the pig. Place another chicken wire sheet over pig and other foods. Spread lots of banana and ti leaves on wire. Completely cover everything with burlap bags presoaked in water, overlapping the bags to extend about one foot beyond rim of hole. Overlap remaining bags to cover hole and top with canvas tarps.

Finally, spread the tarp-covered hole with dirt. Lightly dampen the dirt with water. Watch for any steam leaks, covering with more dirt if necessary.

When the cooking time is over, carefully remove the dirt by scraping it from the canvas with a shovel. Carefully lay back each tarp from top to base. Remove each burlap bag in the same way. Remove the top sheet of chicken wire and banana and ti leaves.

The pig is now carefully lifted out by the wire mesh and the rocks removed from the cavity by the imu tenders. Use tongs to remove the rocks or remove by hand; dunk bare hands in a pail of cold water, reach in and remove each hot rock, toss aside and redunk hands, repeating the process until all rocks are removed.

The pig is then carved and the meat shredded by hand. This is called Kalua pork. It is so ono (good).

Illustrations

Figure 1:   Imu hole, five feet in diameter by three feet deep

Figure 2:   Two-inch pipe placed in hole

Figure 3:   Kindling wood arranged around pipe at bottom of hole

Figure 4:   Firewood stacked on kindling to rim of hole

Figure 5:   Lava rocks piled on firewood, pipe removed and kerosene soaked burlap bag lit and pushed into pipe hole to ignite kindling

Figure 6:   Rocks settled in hole after wood is burned, wood fragments removed and rocks leveled

Figure 7:   Banana stumps and banana and ti leaves placed on rocks

Figure 8:   Pig placed in center of hole with other food. Hole covered with chicken wire sheet and layered, in order, with more banana and ti leaves, burlap, canvas and dirt

(If you no like plenty work, Brah, see phone book under "catering.")

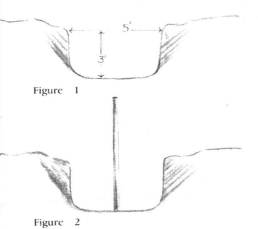

Figure   1

Figure   6

Figure   2

Figure   7

Figure   3

Figure   4

Figure   8

Figure   5

13

POLYNESIAN PRINCE

For the bachelor's farewell, promotion, celebration, graduation, retirement, ordination, wedding rehearsal dinner or going-away get together for college student or military-bound.

Diamondhead Prime Rib Roast
Lobster Tail Lahaina
Fluffy Gourmet Rice
Lehua Salad
Haupia Cake
Iced Tea
Coffee Smoothie

HAWAIIAN PRINCESS

For debutante luncheons, bridal teas, sweet sixteen birthday parties, graduation or going to college farewells . . . a refreshing change from those casserole menus.

Hot Spinach Salad
Bird of Paradise
Fresh Pineapple Mist
Coconut Mousse
Hot Kona Coffee (or quality substitute)

TROPICAL HEAT WAVE
(Teenager's Delight)

To celebrate the coming of spring and those wonderful long days of summer, a luau attuned to teen tastes.

Puka Burgers
Pineapple Outriggers
Surf Baked Beans
Chinese Almond Cookies
Sunset Spritz

For invitations, use a surfing scene and key decorations to the "Tropical Heat Wave" theme.

KEIKI (Little One) LUAU

A wonderful way for children to learn about Hawaii whether they live in the islands, on the mainland or in Canada.

Fresh Pineapple
Rainbow Sparklers
Haupia

Bring the pineapple to the group or class and carve it with the children while discussing the agriculture of the fruit and allowing them to taste, smell and feel it. (Lee says to rinse the mouth or drink water after eating fresh pineapple, but I'm not bothered by the lingering flavors.) After eating the fruit, plant the crown in soil in a clay pot to leave in the classroom.

Provide haupia (coconut pudding) to serve. Crack a coconut, puncturing two of the eyes to drain the liquid. Play background Hawaiian music as you talk about the coconut tree.

Fabulous rainbows are an integral part of the Hawaiian climate. The Rainbow Sparklers will reinforce that image.

Suggest that the class make leis (in advance of their luau) from strips of colorful plastic. If someone in the community is from Hawaii, ask them to assist the children.

Children love their own little luau. I know because I've supervised plenty of these fun-filled educational parties.

See Resources for contacting the Bishop Museum for Hawaiian names for the children and other information. The museum is wonderful about providing the material at a nominal cost. See also **The Hawaiian Name Book** (Bess Press, 1988, $4.95).

PUPU PARTY
Hawaiian Finger Foods

A very special and intimate way to entertain Hawaiian-style, particularly nice for bon voyage or sailing parties or introducing new friends.

Teriyaki Kabob Pupus
Sesame Sherry Sticks
Miniature Drumsticks
Crisp Won Tons
High Voltage Mustard Sauce
Sweet and Sour Sauce
Hawaiian Coconut Nog

The variety of munchables and tidbits that can be served at a pupu party is practically limitless. You can figure ten "bites" per guest and three to four cups of beverage each.

Keep hot foods hot and cold foods cold. Pass hot appetizers straight from the oven, making sure they are easy to handle (not drippy or awkward to pick up).

You may limit your decorating to a Luau Carved Fruit (see index) and a few island brochures secured from a local travel agent. Encourage your guests to dress appropriately and their attire will contribute the rest of the sparkle.

We have used the pupu approach to aloha parties prior to escorting tour groups to Hawaii. It's a great setting for meeting future travel companions.

MAINLAND LUAU

A Hawaiian party to celebrate a special occasion in the lives of friends and loved ones, adapted for mainland setting and food preparation.

Watermelon Basket
Pineapple Outriggers (see Luau Fruit Carvings)
Oven Kalua Pork
Hawaiian Short Ribs
Sweet and Sour Chicken Wings
Smart and Sassy Shrimp
Chicken with Long Rice
Haupia
Banana Nut Bread
Tahitian Ice Cream Cake
Beverage of Choice (see Luau Punches)

Graduations, weddings, birthdays and promotions are events made even more special when you create a little bit of paradise for your guests. This graceful and colorful form of dining and entertainment can be adapted to any setting — an apartment, large home, backyard or poolside. Let your imagination go and have the time of your life!

The success of a luau, whether large or small, comes from the heart and effort of the host and hostess. Good planning is a prerequisite for success and allowing the hosts to relax and enjoy themselves with their guests.

The start of any party is preparing the guest list. The number of guests is limited only to the size of the location. Invitations should emphasize your Hawaiian theme (see Aloha Invitation).

The object of a luau is to have fun, so choose foods which are simple to prepare or may be prepared in advance. We have suggested several menus and recipes which can help you decide. They range from the traditional Hawaiian luau, complete with imu, to simpler menus for modern life styles. Traditional Hawaiian food is not necessary, but you may find it fun to include some dishes from the islands. A luau is perfect for potluck too, with each guest asked to prepare a recipe you have selected.

RECIPES

PUPUS

(Appetizers)

Pupus, Hawaiian finger foods, snacks or appetizers are served generously in the island. Their exotic flavors are extracted from local favorites featuring macadamia nuts, small bits of meat, vegetables and oriental specialties. They are usually served with a zesty sauce. Add a bowl of rice and you have a meal or a menu for a pupu party.

TERIYAKI KABOB PUPUS

1 pound	**sirloin steak or rib-eye steak**
1 (8-ounce) can	**pineapple chunks**
¼ cup	**shoyu (soy) sauce**
1 tablespoon	**sugar**
1 teaspoon	**grated peeled ginger root**
1	**clove garlic, grated**
16	**whole water chestnuts**
16	**stuffed green olives**

Cut meat into 16 cubes about ¾ inch thick. Drain pineapple, reserving syrup. Combine ½ cup syrup, shoyu (soy) sauce, sugar, ginger root and garlic. Pour liquid over meat and marinate for 1 hour, turning occasionally. Using half of barbecue skewer, thread cube of meat, pineapple chunk and water chestnut on each. Broil, 3 inches from heat source, for 5 minutes; turn and broil for 5 minutes. Garnish end of skewer with stuffed olive. Serve piping hot.

Yields 16 kabobs.

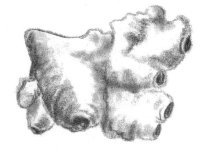

MINIATURE DRUMSTICK

20	chicken wings, about 3 pounds
2 tablespoons	vegetable oil
½ cup	shoyu (soy) sauce
¼ cup	medium or dry sherry
¼ cup	ketchup
2	tablespoons sugar
¼ teaspoon	ground peeled ginger root
	shredded lettuce

Cut wings apart at joints, discarding tips. Fry wings in oil in 5-quart Dutch oven or saucepot, stirring constantly, for about 7 minutes. Reduce heat to medium; add shoyu (soy) sauce, sherry, ketchup, sugar and ginger root, stirring to blend well. Cook, covered, for about 25 minutes, stirring occasionally. Remove cover and cook for additional 10 minutes, stirring frequently, until all liquid is absorbed. Chill, covered, to serve cold on shredded lettuce or serve warm. Drumsticks may be prepared a day in advance and stored in refrigerator.

Yields 40 appetizers.

CRISP WON TON

½ pound	pork, finely ground
¼ teaspoon	sugar
½ teaspoon	shoyu (soy) sauce
2 drops	sesame oil
½ teaspoon	salt
1 stalk	green onion, finely chopped
8	shrimp, chopped
2	water chestnuts, chopped
	black pepper
1 pound	won ton pi

Combine all ingredients except won ton pi. Place ½ teaspoon filling in center of won ton square. Fold in half diagonally, forming a triangle. Moisten edge and seal by firmly pressing edges together. Turn pointed top of triangle to meet fold; turn folded side down. Overlap opposite corners, moisten and press together. Deep fry until brown and crisp. Drain on paper towels. *Continued on next page.*

Note: Illustrations on how to fold a won ton are usually shown on won ton pi package wrappers. Won ton pi are sold in the specialty section of supermarkets or at an oriental food store.

Yields 18 to 24 won tons.

Sesame Sherry Sticks

1 (10 ounce) package	pie crust mix
1 cup	grated cheese
½ cup	sherry
¼ cup	sesame seeds
½ teaspoon	garlic salt

Lightly grease baking sheets. Make pie crust mix according to package directions, adding cheese when mixing crust. Use sherry for liquid instead of water. Shape dough into small sticks, using about 1 teaspoonful of dough for each. Roll sticks in sesame seeds and place about 1 inch apart on prepared baking sheets. Bake at 425 degrees about 8 to 10 minutes. Serve hot or cold. Store cooled sticks in air tight containers.

Makes 3 dozen appetizers.

SWEET AND SOUR SAUCE

½ cup	pineapple juice
½ cup	white wine vinegar
2 tablespoons	peanut oil
2 tablespoons	firmly packed light brown sugar
1 tablespoon	shoyu (soy) sauce
½ teaspoon	freshly ground black pepper
2 teaspoons	cornstarch
4 teaspoons	cold water

Combine pineapple juice, vinegar, oil, sugar, shoyu (soy) sauce and pepper in saucepan; bring to a boil. Dissolve cornstarch in water; add to hot mixture and stir until sauce is clear and slightly thickened.

Yields 1½ cups.

HIGH VOLTAGE MUSTARD SAUCE

3 tablespoons	dry mustard
2 tablespoons	peanut oil
2 tablespoons	water
¼ cup	sugar
1 tablespoon	cornstarch
½ teaspoon	salt
½ cup	water
¼ cup	white vinegar

Combine mustard and oil in small bowl. Gradually add 2 tablespoons water, stirring constantly, to form smooth paste. Stir sugar, cornstarch and vinegar; blend thoroughly. Cook over medium heat, stirring constantly, until thickened. Gradually add to mustard mixture, stirring constantly, until blended. Chill until serving time. Stir before serving and serve at room temperature.

Yields 1 cup. (Very hot! A little goes a long way)

DIAMONDHEAD PRIME RIB ROAST

1 (8-9 pound)	rib roast
	garlic salt
	seasoning salt
	black pepper
	white pepper
1 (8-ounce)	can spiced apple rings, drained
	fresh parsley sprigs

Sprinkle roast on all sides with garlic salt, seasoning salt, black and white pepper; knead into meat (do not punch holes in the roast). Place roast, fat side up, on rack in roasting pan. Insert meat thermometer, making sure the bulb does not touch fat or bone. Bake, uncovered, at 325 degrees, for approximately 3 to 4 hours. Roast to internal temperature of 150 degrees for medium rare and to 160 degrees for medium doneness. Remove from oven. Trim fat from roast. If desired; bake at 400 degrees for 10 minutes or until browned. Slice roast and place slices on hot serving platter. Garnish with spiced apple rings and parsley.

Serves 12-16

PUKA BURGERS

(Puka means hole in Hawaiian)

4 pounds	lean ground beef
	selection of condiments
	in small containers
	chopped onion
	chopped pickles
	relish
	cheese sauce
	ketchup
	mustard
	crushed pineapple
	lettuce, to garnish
	tomato slices, to garnish
	salt and pepper, to taste

Preheat broiler. Using 4 to 5 ounces of meat at a time, shape into patties, forming a hole in center of each. Place under broiler and cook to desired doneness. Place on hot buns and allow each person to select condiments to place in puka (hole). Garnish with lettuce and tomato, if desired. Season with salt and pepper. Kids especially enjoy filling the puka and it gives new zest to the old standby hamburger.

Serves 12 to 16. In Hawaii, be sure to put out the shoyu.

BIRD OF PARADISE

1 (20-ounce) can	Dole® sliced pineapple in syrup
2	chicken breasts, split, or 3-pound fryer, cut up
2 tablespoons	butter
¼ cup	dry sherry
3 tablespoons	shoyu (soy) sauce
2	large cloves garlic, pressed
2 tablespoons	chopped crystallized ginger
½ teaspoons	salt
1	red bell pepper, seeded and cut in chunks
1½ cups	sliced celery
½ cup	sliced green onions
1	papaya, peeled and sliced, optional
1 tablespoon	cornstarch
½ cup	water

Drain pineapple, reserving syrup. Saute chicken in butter; drain excess fat. Combine reserved syrup, sherry, shoyu (soy) sauce, garlic, ginger and salt; pour over chicken. Simmer, covered, for 30 minutes, turning chicken once. Place chicken on platter.

Combine pineapple, pepper, celery, onion and papaya in skillet. Dissolve cornstarch in water; stir into pan juices. Bring mixture to a boil; cook until thickened. Spoon on chicken.

Serves 4

CHICKEN LONG RICE

2 tablespoons	vegetable oil
½ teaspoon	peeled ginger root, crushed
1 clove	garlic, crushed
2 to 3 pounds	fryer chicken or thighs, cut in serving pieces
1 quart	water
6	large fresh mushrooms, sliced
	salt to taste
½ teaspoon	black pepper, optional
½ teaspoon	monosodium glutamate
⅝ teaspoon	curry powder
1 bundle	long rice, soaked until soft and cut in 3-inch lengths
3 stalks	green onion, cut in 2-inch lengths

Heat oil in heavy saucepan. Stir-fry ginger root, garlic and chicken until lightly browned. Add water and mushrooms; cook for about 45 minutes or until chicken is tender. Add salt, pepper, monosodium glutamate and curry; cook for 15 minutes. Stir in long rice and onion; simmer for 10 minutes.

Serves 6-8

CHICKEN OR SQUID LU'AU

7	whole coconuts or 6 cups frozen coconut milk
5 to 6 pounds	chicken thighs or cooked squid
4 teaspoons	salt, divided
6 cups	water, divided
9 pounds	taro leaves

Drain liquid from coconuts into bowl. Crack shell, remove white meal and grate. Measure 4 cups reserved coconut liquid (adding water if necessary), pour over grated coconut and let stand 15 minutes. Squeeze meat and juice through double thickness of dampened cheese cloth into bowl; set aside. Combine chicken, 3 teaspoons salt and 3 cups water in saucepan; simmer until meat is tender. Bone and cut into 1-inch pieces; set aside. If using squid, cut into ½-inch pieces. Remove stem and strip tough part of rib from washed taro leaves. Place leaves, 1 teaspoon salt and 3 cups water in deep saucepan; simmer for 1 hour. Drain and add fresh water; simmer for 1 additional hour or until bitter sting is extracted from leaves. Squeeze to remove excess water. Add meat and coconut milk to taro leaves; heat thoroughly and serve immediately.

Serves 20

EASY CHICKEN LUAU

16	**chicken thighs**
1 teaspoon	**salt**
6 pounds	**frozen leaf spinach, thawed**
2 (12-ounce) cans	**frozen coconut milk**

Place chicken with water to cover in saucepan; season with salt. Simmer for 45 minutes or until chicken is tender. Bone and cut into bite-sized pieces; set aside. Squeeze excess water from spinach. Combine spinach, chicken and coconut milk in saucepan; heat until cooked but do not boil. Serve hot.

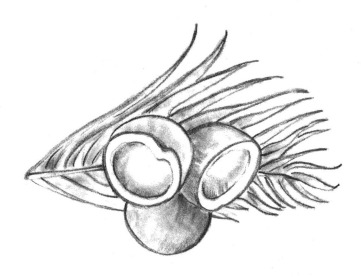

SWEET AND SOUR CHICKEN WINGS

2 pounds	chicken wings
	garlic powder
	salt
	pepper
2	eggs, beaten
	cornstarch
	vegetable oil
1 tablespoon	shoyu (soy) sauce
3 tablespoons	ketchup
½ cup	sugar
¼ cup	vinegar
¾ cup	chicken broth

Cut wings apart at joints, discarding tip sections. Season chicken with garlic powder, salt and pepper. Dip pieces into egg. Roll in cornstarch. Fry in oil until browned. Arrange wings in foil-lined pan. Combine shoyu (soy) sauce, ketchup, sugar, vinegar and chicken broth; pour over chicken. Bake at 350 degrees for 45 minutes to 1 hour, turning wings every 15 minutes.

Serves 6

OVEN KALUA PORK

This is so WikiWiki (quick) and ono (good),
you'll want to serve it for a roast pork dinner.

¼ cup	Hawaiian rock salt
5-6 tablespoons	liquid smoke
8 pounds	pork butt
6-8	ti leaves

Rub rock salt and liquid smoke into pork surface. Wrap meat in leaves; enclose in heavy aluminum foil. Bake, covered, at 500 degrees for ½ hour; reduce to 325 degrees and bake for 3½ hours. Shred meat into bite-sized pieces and serve with roasting liquid. For a different flavor, substitute banana, taro or spinach leaves for ti leaves.
Serves 20

HAWAIIAN SHORT RIBS

6 pounds	short ribs
1½ cups	shoyu (soy) sauce
¼ cup	water
½ cup	sugar
½ teaspoon	monosodium glutamate
1 inch piece	peeled ginger root, mashed
3 tablespoons	brandy or bourbon
1 clove	garlic, mashed

In large saucepan, place short ribs and water to cover; bring to a boil and cook for 1 hour (that's right, 1 hour), remove from heat; cool. Drain liquid; pat meat with paper toweling to dry. Combine remaining ingredients in deep narrow bowl; add ribs and marinate for 2 hours and longer when possible. Grill ribs, about 5 inches above hot coals, until golden brown and crisp.

Serves 6
(If you pre-cook ribs by boiling a long time, they should be done when time to grill.)

FISH BAKED IN TI LEAVES

4 pounds	mullet
¼ cup	Hawaiian rock salt
5	ti leaves

Sprinkle fish with salt. Place fish lengthwise on ti leaf; wrap with additional leaves until covered, securing ends with string or piece of stem. Place wrapped fish on 15 x 10 x 1-inch jellyroll pan. Bake, uncovered, at 350 degrees for 30 to 40 minutes. Place on platter, cut open ti leaves and serve.

Note: Onions may be enclosed with fish in ti leaves.
Serves 20

POKE AKU AND OPIHI

5 pounds   **fresh aku or opihi**
3 pounds   **chopped limu koho or manuea**
                   Hawaiian rock salt to taste
3 to 4 tablespoons   **inamona (Kukui nut paste)**

Remove skin from fish; cut fish into 1-inch cubes. Combine with remaining ingredients. Chill and serve.

Note: Fresh swordfish, squid or octopus may be used. A Korean style poke may be prepared using 3 to 5 seeded chopped Hawaiian chili peppers, 1 bunch green onions chopped, 2 tablespoons toasted sesame seeds, 1 tablespoon sesame oil and 2 tablespoons shoyu (soy) sauce. *Serves 20*

LAULAU

1½ pounds   **salted butterfish or**
                   salted salmon
2½ pounds   **beef brisket or bottom round**
5 pounds   **pork butt**
2 pounds   **pork belly, optional**
200   **taro leaves**
60   **ti leaves**

Soak salted fish in water for ½ hour, changing water twice. Cut fish and beef into 1-inch cubes; cut pork into 1½ to 2 inch cubes; set aside. Remove stems or tough ribs from back of washed ti and taro leaves. Peeled taro leaf stems may be cooked in laulau. Set ti leaves aside. To assemble each laulau, place 10 taro leaves in stack. Place a piece of fish, beef, pork and pork belly in center of each stack. Fold leaves to form a neat bundle. Place 2 ti leaves across each other to form an X. Place a taro bundle on X, folded side down. Bring ends of ti leaf together, pulling tightly over bundle with ends erect. Bring ends of second ti leaf together in same way. Place bundle on a third ti leaf and close in same manner for total coverage of bundle; stems and ends should all be standing up. Holding bundle tightly with one hand, split the stem of a third ti leaf into two lengths; wind stem ties around the stems and ends several times, securing tightly with a knot. Trim remaining stems and ends 3 to 4 inches above knot. Steam laulau for at least 4 hours.

Steaming: The steamer should be large enough to allow the steam to circulate freely. If you do not have a steamer you may use a large porcelain or stainless steel roaster. If the container is too large to replace a lid with space at the top for the steam, then make a domed top of heavy aluminum foil. A 5 gallon container with two racks (one on top of the other) can accommodate 20 average size laulaus.

The water should be boiling when laulau is placed in steamer and kept at a steady boil during the steaming time. This seals in the flavors and the juices. The laulau is placed on a rack (making sure to leave space around each one) 2 to 3 inches from the boiling water. Keep a kettle of boiling water ready to replace any that has boiled away.
Serves 20

(If you're in Hawaii or California, order from a local restaurant that prepares laulau.)

LOBSTER TAIL LAHAINA

2 (1-pound)	**fresh lobster tails**
1½ teaspoons	**salt, divided**
4 cups	**shredded cabbage**
4 stalks	**celery, cut in paper-thin strips**
2	**onions, cut in paper-thin strips**
¼ teaspoon	**pepper**
1 cup	**mayonnaise**
1 tablespoon	**lemon juice**
½ teaspoon	**monosodium glutamate**
4 teaspoons	**mayonnaise, divided**
½ teaspoon	**white pepper**
	dash of paprika

Wash lobster tails and place into boiling water with 1 teaspoon salt. Cook, covered, for 20 minutes. Drain and cool. Remove meat from shell; shred, place in bowl and set aside. In a large bowl, combine cabbage, celery, onion, remaining salt, pepper, 1 cup mayonnaise, lemon juice and monosodium glutamate. Add lobster meat and mix well. Place in 4 to 6 lobster shells or individual baking dishes. Top each with 1 teaspoon mayonnaise, white pepper, and paprika. Bake at 325 degrees (preheated) for 15 minutes.
Serves 4-6.

LOMI LOMI SALMON

1 pound	salted salmon
4 pounds	tomatoes, finely chopped
2 medium	onions, minced
1 cup	crushed ice
1 bunch	green onion, minced

Place salmon in water to cover; soak 2 to 3 hours, changing the water several times. Drain salmon. Remove skin, bones and white strings. Using spoon or fingers, shred salmon into small pieces; place with tomato and onion in bowl. Chill. Cover with thin layer of ice about 1 hour before serving. Add green onion just before serving. If salmon is unsalted, rub with rock salt and let stand overnight; rinse well and soak in water for 1 hour or longer, changing water 2 or 3 times.
Serves 20.

(You can use canned salmon, and get away with it on the mainland.)

SMART AND SASSY SHRIMP

1 (¼-inch) slice	peeled fresh ginger root
1 large clove	garlic, peeled
2 tablespoons	shoyu (soy) sauce
1 tablespoon	dry sherry
2 tablespoons	ketchup
1 teaspoon	sugar
¼ teaspoon	red pepper, optional
2 tablespoons	peanut oil
1 pound	raw shrimp, peeled, deveined and patted dry
2	green onions, including tops, cut diagonally in 1-inch pieces

Mince ginger root and garlic; set aside. Mix shoyu (soy) sauce, sherry, ketchup, red pepper and sugar; set aside. Heat oil in wok or skillet. Stir-fry ginger root and garlic for a few seconds. Discard garlic. Add shrimp and stir-fry for 3 minutes or until pink. Add green onion and stir-fry for 30 seconds. Stir in shoyu (soy) sauce and cook 30 seconds. Stir just to blend ingredients and serve immediately.
Serves 4.

LEHUA SALAD

(My favorite salad — Mae)

2 bunches	spinach, washed, trimmed and torn in bite-sized pieces
1 teaspoon	sugar, divided
6	hard-cooked eggs, chopped
½ pound	ham, julienned
1 (10-ounce) package	frozen petite peas, partially thawed
1	flat round white onion, thinly sliced and separated into rings
1 cup	commercial sour cream
1 cup	mayonnaise
	curry powder, optional
½ pound	Swiss cheese, grated
1 pound	bacon, cooked, drained and crumbled

Arrange half of spinach on bottom of 4-quart shallow glass serving bowl. Sprinkle with ½ teaspoon sugar. Place eggs in layer on spinach; layer ham on eggs. Top with remaining spinach and sprinkle with remaining sugar. Spread peas on spinach; arrange onion on peas. Combine sour cream and mayonnaise, seasoning with curry powder if desired, spread evenly on salad and to edges to seal. Chill, covered, overnight. When ready to serve, sprinkle with cheese and bacon. *Serves 8-10.*

HOT SPINACH SALAD

½ pound	bacon, chopped
2 bunches	spinach, well rinsed
¼ pound	fresh mushrooms, thinly sliced
2	hard-cooked eggs, grated
½ cup	grated Parmesan cheese
	freshly ground black pepper
2 tablespoons	olive oil
3 tablespoons	red wine vinegar
	juice of ½ lemon
1½ teaspoons	Worcestershire sauce

Fry bacon until crisp; drain on absorbent paper, reserving drippings. In large clear glass bowl, combine spinach, mushrooms, egg, bacon, cheese, and pepper; toss lightly to mix. Warm reserved bacon drippings, oil, vinegar, lemon juice and Worcestershire sauce in pan over medium-high heat. Pour dressing over spinach mixture, toss lightly and serve immediately. Sprinkle with additional pepper, if desired.

Serves 2-4.

SURF BAKED BEANS

1 pound (2 cups)	dried navy beans, rinsed
2 quarts	cold water
½ teaspoon	salt
2/3 cup	firmly packed brown sugar
2 teaspoons	dry mustard
¼ cup	molasses
¼ pound	salt pork
1	large onion, sliced

Combine beans and water in large saucepan. Bring to a boil, simmer for 2 minutes, remove from heat and let stand for 1 hour, covered. Stir in salt. Simmer, covered, for about 1 hour or until tender. Drain, reserving liquid to measure 2 cups liquid, adding water if necessary. Mix liquid, sugar, mustard and molasses together. Cut salt pork in half; score one half and grind or thinly slice remainder. Combine beans, onion and ground pork in 2-quart bean pot or casserole. Pour sugar mixture over beans. Top with scored salt pork. Bake, covered, at 300 degrees for 5 to 7 hours, adding more liquid if necessary. For traditional New England baked beans, decrease brown sugar to 1/3 cup and increase molasses to ½ cup.
Serves 8.

GREEN ONIONS WITH ROCK SALT

20	green onions
3 to 4 tablespoons	Hawaiian rock salt
	Hawaiian chili pepper, optional

Trim onions to 6 to 8 inch lengths, leaving some green top. Serve onion and peppers on squares of ti leaves with ½ to 1 teaspoon rock salt for dipping.
Serves 20.

BAKED SWEET POTATOES

10	large sweet potatoes

To cook sweet potatoes (or turkey, chicken or laulau) in imu, shape a separate basket from non-galvanized chicken wire. The size is determined by the number and size of potatoes, chicken or laulau. Arrange in wire basket and place basket above pig in imu.
Serves 20.

FLUFFY GOURMET RICE

¾ cup	white quick-cooking rice
1-1/3 cups	hot chicken broth or bouillon
1 tablespoon	vegetable oil
6	fresh green onions, minced
1/3 cup	sliced fresh mushrooms
1	large tomato, peeled, seeded and chopped
3 tablespoons	chopped pimento
¾ teaspoon	salt (omit if using bouillon)
¼ teaspoon	black pepper
2 tablespoons	slivered toasted almonds
2 tablespoons	sauteed raisins
	paprika

Prepare rice according to package directions, using broth or bouillon for liquid. Heat oil in wok or large saucepan; add onion and cook until soft but not browned. Add mushrooms, tomato and rice; mix well. Season with salt and pepper. Cook, covered, for 3 minutes. Turn off wok heat source or remove saucepan from heat. Toss rice mixture with fork. Add pimento and raisins. Place a paper towel between lid and pan to absorb excess moisture. Add paprika and almonds when ready to serve.
Serves 6-8.

POI

7 pounds	poi
1 to 2 cups	water

Poi should be fresh, 1 or 2 days old. Freeze-dried or bottled poi may be substituted, although the flavor is more bland. Squeeze poi from bag into bowl. Gradually adding water, mix with hands until smooth, the consistency of thick paste. Store, covered, in a cool place. Serve at room temperature. If poi is kept at room temperature for several days, it will gradually become sour. If refrigerated, it will sour more slowly but should be covered with a layer of water. It may be mixed with more water when ready to serve as it hardens when cold.
Serves 20.

BANANA-NUT BREAD

2 cups	flour
2½ teaspoons	baking powder
¼ teaspoon	soda
¼ teaspoon	salt
1 cup	mashed banana
½ cup	butter
¾ cup	sugar
2	large eggs
½ cup	chopped unsalted macadamia nuts

Sift flour, baking powder, soda and salt together. Combine banana, butter and sugar; cream well. Add eggs and dry ingredients to banana mixture. Fold in nuts. Pour into well-greased 9 x 5 x 3 inch loaf pan. Bake at 350 degrees for 50 minutes.
Serves 6-8.

CHINESE ALMOND COOKIES

1 cup	cake flour
¾ cup	powdered sugar
¼ teaspoon	salt
½ cup	finely ground blanched almonds
6 tablespoons	peanut oil
1	egg, well beaten
1 teaspoon	almond extract
	whole blanched almonds

Sift flour, sugar, salt and ground almonds together. Add oil. Stir in egg and extract. Roll dough to about ¼-inch thickness. Cut into small rounds. Press a whole almond in center of each. Bake at 375 degrees for 15 minutes.
Yields 2 dozen.

FRESH PINEAPPLE MIST

1	whole fresh pineapple
¾ cup	ginger ale, chilled
¼ cup	orange juice, chilled
1 tablespoon	lime juice

Remove green top from pineapple and rinse fruit thoroughly. Cut pineapple into quarters. Remove fruit from shell, core and cut into large chunks. Place about 4 pieces in blender and whip at high speed until pureed; repeat with remaining chunks. Combine pureed pineapple, ginger ale and juices in blender; whip on low speed until blended. Pour into tall glasses and garnish with decorated straws and fresh mint leaves. This may also be served in the whole pineapple. Cut a ¼-inch slice from top of the fruit. Using a knife or spoon, gently remove pineapple pulp, leaving shell intact. Proceed with pureeing pineapple and blending with remaining ingredients. Chill until ready to serve. Pour mixture into shell and serve with 2 thin straws and garnish with fresh mint leaf.
Serves 4.

TAHITIAN ICE CREAM CAKE

12	lady fingers, split lengthwise
1 pint	vanilla ice cream, softened
1 (8-ounce) can	crushed pineapple or chopped mangoes

Line bottom of 8 x 8 x 2-inch baking pan with lady fingers. Spread ice cream on lady fingers. Top with fruit. Cut in squares and serve immediately.
Serves 6.

COCONUT MOUSSE

1 pint	half and half milk
3 packages	unflavored gelatin
1/3 cup	water
1 cup	sugar
2 cups	grated moist coconut
1½ pints	whipping cream
1 teaspoon	coconut extract

Pour half and half in saucepan; bring just to a boil. dissolve gelatin in water; add with sugar to half and half and continue cooking until sugar is dissolved. Cool. Add coconut. Beat cream and coconut extract until stiff; fold into coconut mixture. Pour into 8-cup mold. Chill until firm. *Serves 10.*

MALIHINI (NEWCOMER) HAUPIA

1/3 cup	cornstarch
½ cup	sugar
⅛ teaspoon	salt
2 (12-ounce) cans	frozen coconut milk

Combine cornstarch, sugar and salt. Stir in ½ cup coconut milk; blend to form smooth paste. Heat remaining milk and add cornstarch mixture. Cook, stirring frequently, for about 20 minutes or until thickened. Pour into 8 x 8 x 2-inch baking pan. Cool and chill. Cut into 1½-inch squares. Delicious anytime.
Serves 16-24.

HAUPIA CAKE

**(Make an impression
anytime you serve this wonderful cake)**

10	eggs, separated
1 teaspoon	cream of tartar
1¼ cups	sugar, divided
1½ cups	cake flour
1 tablespoon	baking powder
¼ teaspoon	salt
¼ cup	coconut milk or fresh milk
¼ cup	water
½ cup	vegetable oil
1 teaspoon	vanilla flavoring

Beat egg whites and cream of tartar until stiff but not dry. Gradually add ½ cup sugar. Set aside. Sift remaining sugar, flour, baking powder and salt together in a bowl. Make a well in dry ingredients. Add egg yolks, coconut milk, water, oil and vanilla; beat until smooth. Fold yolk mixture into beaten egg whites. Pour into ungreased 13 x 9 x 2-inch

baking pan. Bake at 350 degrees for 30 to 35 minutes. When cake is done, invert on wire rack to cool for about 45 minutes. Spread with Haupia Frosting.
Serves 12-16.

HAUPIA FROSTING

1 (12-ounce) can	**frozen coconut milk**
2 cups	**milk**
½ cup	**sugar**
¼ teaspoon	**salt**
6 tablespoons	**cornstarch**
1½ teaspoons	**vanilla flavoring**
	fresh coconut, shredded

Combine all ingredients, except shredded coconut, in saucepan. Cook over moderate heat, stirring constantly until thickened. Cool. Spread on Haupia Cake and sprinkle with coconut.

LUAU COOLERS, COCKTAILS AND PUNCHES

Exotic beverages add sparkle to a party. Follow these suggestions, add your own ideas and take a bow — your performance as a luau host or hostess will long be remembered.

Waikiki Champagne Punch
Festive Fruit Punch
Honolulu Punch
Pineapple Lime Luau
Pacific Sunset
Mai Tai
Pina Colada

Keep beverages from becoming diluted and lukewarm. Freeze ice blocks in advance to compliment the punch. Placed in the punch bowl, they will keep the drink cold and at full strength. Make a frozen ring of layered limes, pineapple chunks or other fruit. Freeze whole peeled fruit such as pineapple, oranges and lemons. Frozen tomato juice, spiced with pepper sauce, cools a pitcher of Bloody Marys.

Serving containers can be as novel as cored pineapple shells (whole or half) or coconut shells or traditional as clear glass or crystal. Tiki mugs and other decorative glasses are appropriate too. (See Resources.)

None can compete with the Hawaiians when it comes to creative garnishes au naturel. Thread fresh flowers or fruit on one end of a straw or thin bamboo skewer; insert opposite end in drink. Skewer cocktail sticks with strawberries, cherries or citrus peel. Slip small wedges of watermelon, pineapple, orange, apple, lemon or lime on the rim of a glass.

To frost glasses, fill a scooped-out watermelon shell with crushed ice and place glasses, rim side down, in ice. Or place glasses and punch bowl in freezer for a few minutes to make them inviting to the thirsty guest.

Make ice cubes from several different colored fruit drink mixes or place mint leaves, citrus wedges, cherries or strawberries in separate cubicles of ice tray, fill with clear carbonated beverage and freeze.

Coat the rim of a glass with powdered sugar, lemon or lime juice.

For an unusual punch bowl, cut a watermelon such as the Volcano Watermelon (see index).

(Now, as we say in Hawaii, "suck 'em up!")

PINEAPPLE LIME LUAU

1 (46-ounce) can	Dole® pineapple juice
1 (6-ounce) can	frozen lemonade, diluted
	crushed ice
10	orange slices or strawberries
10	mint sprigs

Combine pineapple juice and limeade. Pour over crushed ice in glass. Garnish with orange slice or strawberry and mint sprig.
Serves 10.

PACIFIC SUNSET

1 (6-ounce) can	Dole® pineapple juice
1/3 cup	orange juice
	ice cubes
1 tablespoon	grenadine syrup
1	lime wedge

Combine pineapple and orange juice; pour over ice cubes in glass. Add grenadine and lime wedge.
Serves 1.

PINA COLADA

4 ounce or ½ cup Dole® pineapple juice
3 ounce rum
2 ounce coconut cream
2 cups crushed ice

Pour all ingredients into blender. Blend at high speed briefly. Strain into glass and serve.
Serves 2.

MAI TAI

1 (6-ounce) can Dole® pineapple juice
2 tablespoons light rum
2 tablespoons dark rum
1 tablespoon orange-flavored liqueur
1 tablespoon lime juice
crushed ice

Combine juice, rum and liqueur. Fill two 6-ounce glasses with crushed ice. Pour Mai Tai over ice.
Serves 3.

CHI CHI

½ cup Dole® pineapple juice
3 tablespoons tequila
1 tablespoon orange-flavored liqueur
1 lemon wedge, squeezed
crushed ice
1½ tablespoons grenadine

Mix pineapple juice, tequila, liqueur, lemon juice and crushed ice; pour into glass and stir. Slowly add grenadine and allow to settle.
Serves 1.

WAIKIKI CHAMPAGNE PUNCH

2 (46-ounce) can	Dole® pineapple juice, chilled
2 (750-ml) bottles	dry champagne, chilled
2 cups	Chenin Blanc, chilled
1 (20-ounce) can	pineapple chunks in juice
	ice cubes
1 pint	strawberries, sliced
1	orange, thinly sliced
1	lemon, thinly sliced
	mint sprigs

Combine pineapple juice, champagne, wine and undrained pineapple chunks in large punch bowl. Add ice cubes. Float strawberry, orange and lemon slices and mint on punch.
Yields 1½ gallons.

FESTIVE FRUIT PUNCH

1 (46-ounce) can	Dole® pineapple juice
1 (10-ounce) package	frozen raspberries
1 (6-ounce) can	frozen pink lemonade concentrate, undiluted
¼ cup	grenadine syrup
1 quart	lemon-lime flavored carbonated beverage, chilled
	lemon slices
	ice cubes

Combine juice, raspberries, lemonade and grenadine in large punch bowl. Add carbonated beverage just before serving. Garnish with lemon slices and chill with ice cubes.
Yield 3 quarts.

HAWAIIAN COCONUT NOG

1 (8 ½-ounce) can	cream of coconut
1 (13-ounce) can	evaporated milk
1 cup	cola-flavored carbonated beverage
½ teaspoon	vanilla flavoring
1 cup	sugar
4	eggs
	maraschino cherries, optional

Combine cream of coconut, milk, cola, vanilla, sugar and eggs in blender container; blend until smooth. Chill until ready to serve. Garnish each serving with 1 cherry.
Yields 1 quart.

RAINBOW SPARKLERS

**(This one is for Beau, Lauren and Meryl —
our grandchildren)**

3 quarts	water, divided
1 (1-ounce) pkg. ea. of	grape, lime and cherry flavored powdered artificially sweetened drink mixes
2 (2-liter) bottles	lemon-lime carbonated beverage, chilled

Using a large pitcher, combine 1 quart water and grape powdered mix; stir. Fill divided ice trays with all of liquid. Freeze. Repeat with lime and cherry powdered mixes. To serve, fill clear plastic cups with an ice cube of each color. Pour carbonated beverages over cubes. Serve with a colorful straw. Children love to join in to help make this drink. When the cubes begin to melt, the drink looks like a rainbow.
Yields 1½ gallons.

SUNSET SPRITZ

fresh fruit: choice of lemon, lime, cherries, strawberries, maraschino cherries or pineapple chunks or a combination

1 (2-liter) bottle   lemon-lime carbonated beverage or ginger ale

Slice fruit into bite-sized pieces. Place 1 piece of fruit in each cubicle of an ice tray. Fill with sweetened water or clear beverage and freeze until firm. To serve, fill tall clear glasses with 6 to 8 fruit cubes and pour in carbonated beverage. Garnish with fresh pineapple slice, lemon or lime wedge or miniature umbrella. Fruit cubes may be made in advance and stored in freezer.

Yields approximately 2 quarts.

HONOLULU PUNCH

1 (20-ounce) can	pineapple chunks in juice
1 (46-ounce) can	Dole® pineapple juice
3 cups	orange juice
½ cup	fresh lemon juice
1 quart	ginger ale
1 pint	strawberries, stemmed and halved

Pour pineapple chunks and juice into square pan or ice cube trays; freeze. Chill remaining ingredients. Combine frozen pineapple chunks, juices and ginger ale in large punch bowl. Add strawberries to punch. *Yields 1 gallon.*

COFFEE SMOOTHIE

2 cups	strong Kona coffee, cold
2	bananas, optional
1 pint	coffee-flavored ice cream, softened

Blend coffee, bananas and ice cream in blender for 30 seconds or until smooth.
Serves 4.

KONA COFFEE

The Big Island of Hawaii boasts the only commercial coffee plantation in the United States. Homegrown and roasted coffee beans are produced to become the much sought after gourmet-status Kona coffee. It can be found in gourmet shops or specialty delicatessens.

LUAU FRUIT CARVINGS

Can you imagine a luau without carved fruit? Creative paring and arranging of lush tropical fruit can lend an imaginative, colorful tone to the luau table.

Watermelon Basket

I have a friend who is an expert with watermelon baskets, carving and filling and adding the extra touches. She shares her ideas.

A long slender melon is best suited for a basket. If a round melon is used, first cut a thin slice from one side so the melon will sit without rolling.

Cut melon in shape of basket, measuring from end to end, to center the handle. Edges may be straight, notched or scalloped, using a tea cup as a guide.

Remove melon meat, then refill with bite-sized chunks. Add chunks of honeydew melon, cantaloupe and red, green and purple grapes. Arrange clusters of the grapes on the mound of fruit. Chill. Just before serving, add 2 cups of a chilled clear carbonated beverage.

Volcano Watermelon

Cut a thin slice from one end of melon so it will not roll, being careful not to cut through the rind. Cut an opening at the opposite end, carving a scalloped or notched edge.

Remove melon meat and fill with punch. Or leave about half of meat in shell and add honeydew melon, cantaloupe and watermelon fruit balls. Strawberries and blackberries add contrast and more flavor.

The melon may be placed on a tray and the bottom surrounded with pieces of fruit for a lovely and unusual centerpiece.

Honey of a Honeydew

Cut a honeydew melon in half, carving the edges in a zigzag pattern. Scoop out melon meat and toss with combination of cantaloupe, papaya and pineapple chunks, banana sections (dipped in lemon juice to preserve color), strawberries and blueberries. Arrange fruit in melon shells.

PINEAPPLE PEACOCK

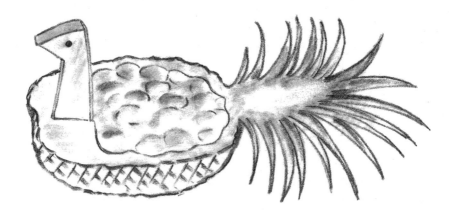

Pineapple Peacock (Continued)

Select a large fresh pineapple with very fresh green leaves. Keep in mind that the pineapple is as ripe on picking as it will ever be, so fragrance and appearance are good guidelines in selecting fruit.

Cut the pineapple in half from top to bottom, including the leafy top. Carefully cut and scoop fruit from center; remove core and carve a bird-shaped head and neck from fruit.

Insert two round toothpicks in bottom of neck and secure to cut surface of pineapple shell near base. Refill cavity with bite-sized chunks of fresh pineapple, lime slices and strawberries.

A tiny lei can be created from bits of cloth. Cut eyes from pieces of lime peel or strawberry and secure to head with fragment of toothpick.

One pineapple can be used to make 2 peacocks.

(This is an attractive centerpiece. I've used it on television presentations and the peacock received rave reviews.)

OUTRIGGER

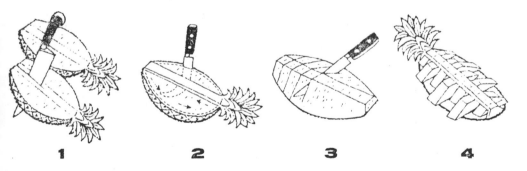

1   **2**   **3**   **4**

Pineapple Outrigger
(Dole®)

Quarter the pineapple from bottom to top, leaving a section of the leafy crown on each piece. Loosen fruit by cutting under and around the core but without removing the core.

Insert knife close to rind and loosen fruit from rind. Remove the fruit and cut crosswise slices. Slip sections of fruit back into shell, under the core, and arrange in a staggered pattern.

THIS LITTLE PIGGIE
WENT TO THE LUAU

Chef Levi Ezell, a member of the elite American Academy of Chefs, shares some of his expert ideas on roasting a suckling pig and keeping it intact.

Obtain a 30 to 40 pound pig from the meat packing plant. It should be fully prepared for cooking. Ask the plant to cut slits in the sides and position the feet.

The night before roasting, store the pig, back side down on a large tray, in a commercial refrigerator. Using salt, white pepper, granulated garlic and thyme, rub each seasoning separately into cavity and then on the outer skin. Using hands, rub vegetable oil onto outer skin and into cavity.

Wrap the ears, feet and tail with aluminum foil. Stuff the cavity and open mouth with foil crunched tightly into balls.

To roast, position suckling with legs down on large roasting tray. Bake at 300 degrees in a commercial oven for approximately 2½ to 3 hours.

Transfer to an open pit, preparing for cooking with mesquite or keawe wood and charcoal. (Chef Ezell prefers the drum type made from barrels.) Place suckling directly on grill.

Because the suckling is already about three-fourths cooked, it will need just 45 minutes to an hour over the wood and coals to achieve optimum flavor. About 15 minutes before removing pig from grill, remove foil from feet, ears and tail to assure even browning.

Carefully remove pig to display tray. If cavity collapses, stuff with iceberg lettuce. Immediately place traditional apple in mouth after removing foil. Insert cherry tomatoes in eye sockets.

Garnish with endive and fresh fruit such as pineapple, kiwi and orange slices, and nontoxic ferns and flowers.

To carve, begin on the ham section at the back, working forward toward the head. To keep the suckling whole for display, serve sliced Boston pork butt prepared the same way and arranged around the cooked suckling.

The preparation of the suckling should be a joint effort. It's not considered fair to sample the pig before the guests arrive. Some may be reluctant to taste but it only takes one slice to convince them!

LET'S GET ORGANIZED

Thoughtful planning and organization will add an atmosphere of leisurely elegance to your hospitality.

Guests feel more at ease and less compelled to offer help if you don't occasionally appear from the kitchen with beaded brow and furrowed forehead.

Planning is imperative. Enthusiasm will override anxiety if preparations are orderly and logical. Develop a time schedule, advising others if they are to be part of the activities. A schedule allows the host or hostess to "dress" the party as painstakingly as themselves.

For very large luaus requiring the assistance of other people, have pre-parties such as ohana (family) get-togethers to create an air of camaraderie and feeling of intimacy.

Party Checklist

These suggestions, plus your own creativity, will help create a little corner of Hawaii no matter where you live.

1. Select menu
   a. Identify recipes and make shopping lists
   b. Note foods to be prepared in advance and frozen
   c. List serving dishes and pieces
2. Make guest list
3. Design invitations
4. Develop a schedule
   _____ time
   _____ place
   _____ invitations
   _____ addressing and mailing
   _____ shopping
   _____ gathering decorations and other items
   _____ delegate tasks when possible
   _____ final preparation
5. Hawaiians love to say "just hang loose" — so enjoy yourself at your luau!

Arrangements List

Tiki torches and fuel
Fresh and imitation flowers
Leis, fresh or imitation
Greenery
Scented candles
Games (board games, cards, frisbees, etc.)
Hawaiian music
Picnic tables
Throw pillows
Straw mats
Paper plates, cups, napkins
Plastic forks, knives, spoons
Bamboo plate and cup holders
Hibachi for cooking appetizers
Coils to repel insects
Film for camera
Entertainment

ALOHA INVITATIONS

Fold a sheet of white or colored 8½ x 11-inch paper into thirds or fourths. Write or type party information so it will appear on the inside of the invitation before folding.

Color the edge of the paper with a felt-tip marker in a color to match the luau theme. Border envelopes with the same color.

Illustrate the outside or front fold of the invitation with a drawing from this book or one of your own.

(Note: It's a good idea to select your envelope first, so you can fold your paper accordingly.)

SETTING THE MOOD

An attractive tropical setting will establish the right atmosphere for your Hawaiian luau theme. Use as much greenery as you can find; ferns, palms, ficus or local green plants add a lush look.

Orchids or local seasonal blossoms are beautiful as table decoration, floated in bowls of water or pinned in the ladies' hair. Hawaiian luaus have fern fronds or ti leaves scattered all over the table with a flower by each place setting.

Tiki torches and candles add to the exotic mood. Tiki torches may be purchased or rented. It has been our experience that kerosene is a better fuel than the more expensive tiki torch fuel.

If properly prepared, the torches should provide hours of flickering light. Be sure to soak the wicks thoroughly in the fuel before immersing in the fuel container. Ignite about an hour in advance to burn off excess kerosene odor.

Scented candles also add to the party decor. They can be floated in the pool (in frisbees covered with foil) or in large bowls of water as centerpieces. You may wish to turn off the pool pump so the candles will float freely. A nice touch in the powder room is to float candles in the bathtub, shutting the glass shower door to create a diffused glow.

For seating, tables and chairs can be used or straw mats placed on the ground. Large floor pillows make casual yet comfortable seating indoors. Hawaiians help themselves to the floor for genuine comfort.

Buffet style service saves wear and tear on the host or hostess and allows the guests to make their own food selections.

Cover the tables with long strips of butcher paper and use colorful paper goods. After the luau, you can simply remove the items to be kept, roll up the paper and toss away.

Luau entertainment depends on location and budget. Hawaiian music is an integral part of the luau. If possible, use live musicians; otherwise play tapes and records of Hawaiian melodies. (See Resources.)

Hula dancers add authenticity. Often they can be hired for a nominal cost through local dance schools.

Audience participation is fun. Many family luaus in Hawaii begin in late afternoon so guests can play volleyball or take a dip in the pool before dark. Hawaiians love games; so board games and cards are often pulled out for play after dinner.

Other entertainment possibilities are prizes for the most authentically dressed, an amateur band of musically-talented guests or a hula contest.

Not to be overlooked is cooperation from Mother Nature, especially if your luau is to be held outdoors. A balmy evening certainly enhances the party. Check the calendar for a half to full moon and schedule accordingly. Set up an alternating location indoors or rent a tent if the weather appears unpredictable.

More Ideas for Large Luaus

If you are planning a large scale luau for friends, club or company, here are some additional suggestions. Remember, the main objective of all luau hospitality is to "hang loose" and enjoy yourself, enriching friendships and creating wonderful memories.

Exotic decorating is easy when you use greenery, water and flowers lavishly to establish the island feeling.

The entryway introduces the mood. Place palm trees at either side. Recruit a pretty girl and handsome man to greet guests in the Hawaiian tradition by placing a lei around each guest's neck and kissing them on the cheek. The greeters should wear Hawaiian attire as should the catering staff and band.

Decorate the food service area and bandstand. Hang potted plants, garland and "aloha" banners from the ceiling. Trellises adorned with tropical birds, flowers and greenery attractively accent the bandstand or head table.

In a large room such as a cafeteria, use fishnet to decorate ceilings and corners. Hang shells, paper fish and glass floats from the nets. Lightweight tissue paper decorations in tropical motif look great dangling from light fixtures. Structural supports such as columns can be disguised as palm trees when they are wrapped in burlap and have palm fronds attached to the top.

Tables can be covered with tapa paper, tropical wrapping paper or tablecloths in splashy prints. Place tissue or real pineapples along the center of tables.

Tables can be improvised from sheets of plywood, supported by bricks or concrete blocks. Seats can be any type of cushion or covered foam pads.

A nice touch is to give tables and private dining areas Hawaiian names such as "Surf's Up Inn," "Kona Wind," "Waikiki Lanai," "Tiki Tiki Wiki," "Chi Chis," "Diamondhead Inn" and so on. (See glossary for more names.)

The head of ceremonies can call two or three tables at a time to the food line (or for other activities); he may translate the name of the tables and possibly even mispronounce the words, adding humor to the occasion.

The bar area may also deserve a name such as "Hang Loose Louie's" or "Diamondhead Lounge."

An artificial pool can be constructed from a child's wading pool. Cover edges with grass matting, fill with water and float flowers in it. Attach floral arrangements to styrofoam for a bigger impact.

Grass shacks can be created by covering wood frames with wire mesh, then attaching hay, palmetto leaves, banana leaves or other large leaves to the wire.

Kahilis are symbols of Hawaiian royalty and make striking decorations for the buffet table, entry or bandstand. Use broom handles or wooden poles of the same size. Attach an empty 5-gallon cardboard ice cream container to one end. Wrap the container with colorful leis. Stand the pole upright.

For the greatest authenticity, use Hawaii's royal colors of red and yellow for the leis and ribbons. All kahilis in Hawaii are those colors and are usually made of feathers.

Finally, don't overlook the restrooms. Identify them with "kane" for men and "wahini" for ladies. Or place cut-outs of a woman in a hula skirt and a man in lava lava (wrap shorts) on the appropriate doors.

Luau Extraordinary

Time, space and money no consideration?

Set tables indoors and out. Color key the theme with hundreds of tropical flowers, either flown in from neighboring islands or, if on the mainland, from Hawaii.

Make orchids the theme. Have the hostess and other ladies of the family wear white or lavender or deep purple dresses with matching shirts for the gentlemen, servers and musicians.

Set tables with stark white cloths and use shades of purple in the napkins and centerpieces to pick up the color in the throat of the orchid. Contrast with fresh green ti leaves on every table.

Shelter the outdoor tables beneath giant umbrellas of the same color. Garnish frosted drinks with miniature white, lavender or deep purple dendrobium orchids. Put some of the flowers into the pool and float others in crystal bowls.

What a splendid picture!

Similar decorations can emerge from a salmon and seafoam green color theme, using birds of paradise as the focal flower.

This writer adores a rainbow theme. The multi-colored arcs sweep the sky almost daily in the islands.

Borrow the color scheme from the streaking hues of the rainbow, selecting tablecloths of bright yellow. Individualize with a wide streamer in red, purple, hot pink or frothy green. Coordinate napkins and centerpieces — mounds of fresh flowers in clay pots — to each table's colors.

Use stark white china and sterling silver. Repeat the colors in your own attire, as well as that of the servers and musicians.

Offer only soft colored floral leis of one color per strand or you may want to greet guests with nosegays.

Food and Flowers

In Hawaii, flowers play a full complementary role to food, whether adorning a simple breakfast plate or the most elegant affair. Fragrant blossoms are plucked daily from the earth and used lavishly as table decorations and food garnishes.

Guests wear flowers in their hair and garlands around their necks, wrists or ankles. The lei is rooted in an attitude of aloha. The full fresh clusters of blossoms, buds, seeds and anise scented leaves are laced together to form a circle of sweet fragrance.

The Hawaiian lei is more than a floral necklace given with a kiss. It is a spirit of thankfulness as each blossom is picked from the good earth and strung, one by one. The care inherent in its creation and the benevolent spirit of its presentation are symbolic of aloha.

The story goes that the lei-cum-kiss began in World War II when an entertainer dared to kiss an officer when presenting him with a lei. Embarrassed, she gave the excuse that it was a Hawaiian tradition, thus starting the lei greeting and kiss custom.

Novelty Leis

Not all leis are made of flowers. Brightly wrapped hard candy (with extra paper on each end) can be tied together with narrow paper ribbon. Wrapped fortune cookies, bubble gum and packages of gum can be used. Cut pieces of net into squares, wrap sweets in square and secure with cord. A nice lei length is 3 feet.

When we fly out of Honululu, our youngest son receives candy or gum leis from his cousins. We consume David's leis, but our floral ones are left to dry according to the folklore that so doing will bring good luck.

Over Which Ear Do I Wear My Flower?

It is Hawaiian tradition for ladies to wear flowers in their hair; the exact location reputedly signals to men where they stand in matters of romance.

If a lady is "taken," she wears a flower over her left ear, the same side as her heart. She wears the flower on the right side if she is available.

A wise wag once told me that if a woman is "taken" but still looking or if she has simply run out of luck, the flower goes on top of her head!

Lighthearted Fashion

The very practicality of Hawaiian fashion makes it inviting to wear. Old meets new in nearly all designs.

Many pattern companies offer easy-to-sew designs in the casual apparel and swim wear sections.

Choose a tropical print for the muumuu. Add a colorful lei and tuck a flower in the hair (over the correct ear). Let yourself go — you're safe in a muumuu!

The lingerie department of local stores is a good source for luau wear as they often sell loosely-fitted casual items in bright tropical prints.

An easy outfit for ladies is a grass skirt worn over a one or two-piece swimsuit. Add a pretty flower in the hair and a floral anklet, go barefoot and strut your stuff, because you'll be the life of the party.

The Pareau (Pe-ri-o)

The pareau is also popularly known as a sarong. It's always been one of Hawaii's most popular fashions. Worn many different ways — long, short or very short — it conveys the longstanding attitude of casualness.

Not only is the pareau beautiful and comfortable, but it is practical as it can also be used for beachwear, shopping, lounging or entertaining. It may be worn with or without a belt. On the back cover, I'm wearing a pongee (Hawaiian silk) pareau.

Selvage

Crosswise
Fold

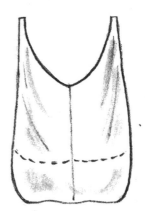

To make a pareau, choose a soft silky or crisp cotton fabric in sizzling colors. Make your "pattern" from newspaper. Then adjust it for length and width.

Cut out as indicated in drawing. Finish edges with a ⅛″ hem. For a more tailored look and even better fit make a seam down the center of back and sew a 3″ dart on each side of the seam.

Make a belt of the same fabric 60″ long and 1 to 2″ wide. Tie around your street-length pareau. You may also feel more comfortable wearing it with your long style as well.

The drawing here fits sizes approximately 8-16.

If you can tie a knot, you can wear a pareau. See the illustrations provided.

Different Ways You Can Tie a Pareau

Buffet Service

Luaus are most frequently served buffet style. These suggestions will make it most convenient and efficient for guests.

Food should be arranged in a thoughtful sequence as the guest has only one free hand once he's picked up his plate. Any dish requiring two serving utensils, such as meat, should be first in order, followed by the plates and then the remaining dishes.

A complete set of flatware should be wrapped in a napkin and secured with a ribbon, pipe cleaner or colored rubber band. The flatware should be at the end of the buffet table as the final item to be picked up.

Place cards on the table to indicate where dishes will be located and the serving pieces which will be used. If possible, splurge and employ someone to assist with last-minute details and service. With cards in place, the server will know where to set the food.

Provide a steady dining surface. If your table is being used for the buffet, then provide television trays or card tables for individual guests. Plate balancing can lead to a food-splattered guest or a stained carpet. Use picnic tables outdoors.

Have the server circulate with a tray of poured drinks such as tea and coffee. Then offer the bread. Let guests help themselves to dessert and coffee, placed on a separate table.

Even if you have to borrow from friends and neighbors, be sure to have plenty of salt and pepper shakers. In Hawaii, you'll need extra containers of shoyu (soy) sauce.

In summary, DON'T AGONIZE — ORGANIZE.

Greeting Guests with Aloha

Be prepared with drinks in frosted glasses or cups (and for non-drinkers, a pretty garnished fruit punch).

Always greet guests with a lei, a hug and one kiss, and a drink, then usher them into the party. Introduce shy or new guests to someone you know will make them feel comfortable and who will continue the introductions to others. Nothing can intimidate a person more at a party than walking into a crowd of strangers without someone to assist in making the guest feel at ease.

Herein lies your charm.

IF THE ALOHA SPIRIT REMAINS CONSTANT AND IS GENEROUSLY GIVEN, IT RETURNS TO YOU AS SURELY AS THE WAVES ON THE SUNSET BEACH.

Mae and Lee Keao

GLOSSARY OF
HAWAIIAN WORDS

The State of Hawaii is the only one to boast its own language. When spoken correctly, it is melodic and beautiful. The Hawaiian alphabet consists of 12 letters: the vowels A, E, I, O and U and the consonants H, K, L, M, P, W.

Alii	— chief, queen, noble
aloha	— hello, goodbye, love
hula	— dance, entertain
kaukau	— food
keiki	— child
lanai	— patio, porch
mahalo	— thanks
malihini	— stranger, newcomer, guest
haole	— formerly any foreigner, now mostly a reference to Caucasian mainlanders
lei	— floral necklace
wahini	— female
kane	— male
tutu	— auntie or grandma
kapuna	— elder, ancestor

The Islands

Hawaii
Kahoolawe
Lanai
Maui
Molokai
Oahu
Kauai
Niihau

RESOURCES are provided for readers' convenience. Correspondence should be direct with the supplier and not to BESS PRESS.

Luau items and fresh flowers

ORCHIDS OF HAWAII INTERNATIONAL, INC.
3703 Provost Avenue
Bronx, New York 10466
(212) 654-7630 in NY
(800) 223-2124

FRESH PINEAPPLE & PAPAYA
Pineapple of Hawaii
2270 Kalakaua Avenue
Suite 1514
Honolulu, Hawaii
1-800-922-4953

Music

Hawaian Records and Tapes
P.O. Box 1342
Kanoehe, Hawaii 96744

Beau Sterling
Nahele Records
P.O. Box 2122
Pearl City, Hawaii 96782

Live entertainment and other Luau services

THE BAREFOOT HAWAIIAN
1401 East Oakton Street
Des Plaines, Illinois 60018
(312) 699-7336

William Keoniana Kelly
1189 W. 1340 North
Orem, Utah 84057
(801) 225-6244

Hawaii Aloha Luau Services
940 Riverside Drive
Pasadena, MD 21122
(301) 437-1949

Luau Fashions

THE BAREFOOT HAWAIIAN
1401 East Oakton Street
Des Plaines, Illinois 60018
(312) 699-7336

General Information on Hawaii

Bernice P. Bishop Museum
P.O. Box 19000-A
1525 Bernice Street
Honolulu, Hawaii 96817

More easy Island recipes and menus

HAWAIIAN MAGIC
Bess Press
P.O. Box 22388
Honolulu, Hawaii 96822

INDEX

# NOTES

 NOTES

# NOTES

 NOTES

# NOTES

 NOTES

 NOTES

 NOTES

NOTES

Reorder
Additional Copies

Share the magic of paradise with friends, clients and associates.

Just order and leave the shipping to us.

ORDER BLANK

Please send me _____ **copies of** *THE HAWAIIAN LUAU BOOK*
@ $8.50 each*.

I am enclosing my check or money order for $_____ **,
payable to BESS PRESS.**

_____

Name (Please Print)

_____

Address

_____

City   State   Zip

*Price includes tax and handling charge. Allow 6-8 weeks for delivery.

**BESS PRESS
P.O. BOX 22388
HONOLULU, HI 96822**